DAZZLING
DIVISION

Also in the Magical Math series

~~~~~~~~~~~~~~~~~~~~~~~~~~~~~~~~~~

Marvelous Multiplication

And coming soon

~~~~~~~~~~~~~~~~~~~~~~~~~

Fabulous Fractions
Measurement Mania

Magical Math

DAZZLING
DIVISION

Games and Activities
That Make Math Easy and Fun

Lynette Long

John Wiley & Sons, Inc.

York • Chichester • Weinheim • Brisbane • Singapore • Toronto

Copyright © 2000 by Lynette Long. All rights reserved
Illustrations copyright © 2000 by Tina Cash-Walsh.

Published by John Wiley & Sons, Inc.
Published simultaneously in Canada

Design and production by Navta Associates, Inc.

The publisher and the author have made every reasonable effort to ensure that the experiments and activities in this book are safe when conducted as instructed but assume no responsibility for any damage caused or sustained while performing the experiments or activities in the book. Parents, guardians, and/or teachers should supervise young readers who undertake the experiments and activities in this book.

ISBN 0-471-36983-7

Printed in the United States of America

10 9 8 7 6 5 4 3 2 1

Contents

1

THE MAGIC OF DIVISION

Once you understand what division is, you'll find it much easier to solve division problems. In this section, you'll learn how to write a division problem, and the names of the parts of a division problem. You'll also look at division in three different ways: division as grouping, division as repeated subtraction, and division as the opposite of multiplication. All of these exercises will help you understand division and prepare you for learning division facts.

Anatomy of a Division Problem

What is division? How do you write a division problem? How do you read one? What are you actually doing when you divide one number by another? Once you can answer these questions, you are well on your way to discovering the magic of division.

There are four basic operations in mathematics: addition, subtraction, multiplication, and division. Division is usually taught last since it is the hardest to master, but learning to divide is just as important as learning to add, subtract, or multiply.

Each of the four basic operations can be expressed as a symbol. The plus sign ($+$) tells you to add two numbers together. The minus sign ($-$) tells you to subtract one number from another. The multiplication sign ($\times$) tells you to multiply one number by another. The division sign ($\div$) tells you to divide one number by another. The problems $6 + 4$, $6 - 4$, 6×4, and $6 \div 4$ are different problems that have different answers.

There are other ways to indicate division besides using the division sign. Sometimes a division problem is written in the form $8\overline{)6,424}$. This problem is read as six thousand, four hundred twenty-four divided by eight. The problem $2\overline{)222}$ is two hundred twenty-two divided by two. And $10\overline{)5}$ is five divided by ten.

3

You can also write a division problem by using a slant line, /. The problem 12/3 is twelve divided by three. You can read 164/4 as one hundred sixty-four divided by four. Or you could write fifty-two divided by twenty-six as 52/26.

One more way to indicate division is with a bar. Twelve divided by four would be written as $\dfrac{12}{4}$, and $\dfrac{14,955}{5}$ would be read as fourteen thousand, nine hundred fifty-five divided by five.

You can write the same division problems five different ways.

✔ thirty-two divided by four

✔ 32 ÷ 4

✔ $4\overline{)32}$

✔ 32/4

✔ $\dfrac{32}{4}$

Now that you know how to write division problems, it's time to find out the names of the three parts of a division problem. Look at the problem 24 ÷ 3. Read this problem as twenty-four divided by three. The number 24 is called the "dividend" (the number to be divided), and the number 3 is called the "divisor" (the number by which the dividend is divided). The answer to the problem (in this case, 8) is called the "quotient" (the number resulting from dividing one number by another).

$$\text{dividend} \div \text{divisor} = \text{quotient}$$

$$\text{divisor} \,\overline{)\,\text{dividend}}^{\,\text{quotient}}$$

$$\text{dividend}/\text{divisor} = \text{quotient}$$

$$\frac{\text{dividend}}{\text{divisor}} = \text{quotient}$$

What are the parts of $42 \div 6 = 7$?

    42 is the dividend

    6 is the divisor

    7 is the quotient

Try a different format. What are the parts of $10/2 = 5$?

    10 is the dividend

    2 is the divisor

    5 is the quotient

Identify the parts of this problem: $6\overline{)132}$.

    132 is the dividend

    6 is the divisor

    The quotient is not given.

Remember this problem is read as one hundred thirty-two divided by six. It is *not* six divided by one hundred thirty-two, even though the 6 is written first.

Here is a coded message. Match the answers to the division problems in the list to the number-letter codes here to spell a word and see how well you understand dividends, divisors, and quotients.

1 = A, 2 = B, 3 = C, 4 = D, 5 = E, 6 = F, 7 = G,

8 = H, 9 = I, 10 = J, 11 = K, 12 = L, 13 = M, 14 = N,

15 = O, 16 = P, 17 = Q, 18 = R, 19 = S, 20 = T,

21 = U, 22 = V, 23 = W, 24 = X, 25 = Y, 26 = Z

1. What is the divisor in the problem fifteen divided by five equals three?

2. What is the dividend in the problem $24 \div 6 = 4$?

3. What is the divisor in the problem $12/3 = 4$?

4. What is the quotient in the problem $30 \div 6 = 5$?

5. What is the dividend in the problem $4\overline{)12}$?

6. What is the quotient in the problem sixty divided by five equals twelve?

7. What is the divisor in the problem $\dfrac{10}{5} = 2$?

8. What is the quotient in the problem $56/4 = 14$?

9. What is the divisor in the problem $20\overline{)20} = 1$?

Did you spell a word? EXCELLENT!

Division is an essential mathematical skill. You will use division every day of your life, so start practicing and soon you'll become a division master. Then you can proudly display the division master certificate at the back of this book.

Division as Grouping

2

Try this tasting activity to learn what division really means. Division is the process of dividing items into equal groups. The dividend tells you how many things you are dividing into equal groups. The divisor tells you how many groups you are dividing these things into. The quotient tells you how many items are in each group.

> ## MATERIALS
>
> 12 cookies
> (or crackers,
> pretzels, raisins,
> or any other
> snack)
>
> large serving
> plate
>
> 12 small plates

Procedure

1. Put the twelve cookies on the serving plate. Put two small plates on the table. You are going to divide the twelve cookies between two imaginary guests to solve the division problem 12 ÷ 2. The number of cookies (12) is the dividend. The number of plates (2) is the divisor. Divide the cookies equally between the two smaller plates. Remember, each guest has to get exactly the same number of cookies. How many cookies are on each plate? If you split the cookies equally, there should be six cookies on each plate. Twelve divided by two is six.

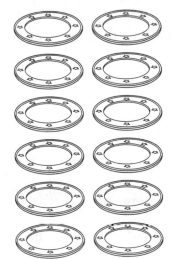

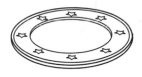

7

2. Place the twelve cookies back on the serving plate. (Don't eat any!) Now place three small plates on the table. You are going to solve the problem 12 ÷ 3. In this problem, 12 is the dividend and 3 is the divisor. Split the cookies equally among the three plates. There should be four cookies on each plate. Twelve divided by three is four.

3. Put the cookies back on the serving plate again and put four small plates on the table. Divide the cookies up. How many cookies does each guest get if each gets the same number? Each guest gets three cookies. Twelve divided by four is three.

4. Return the cookies to the serving plate. Set the table for six guests. Now divide the cookies among these six guests. Each guest gets only two cookies. Oh, well. Twelve divided by six is two.

5. Finally, set the table for twelve guests. Divide the cookies fairly among the twelve guests. Each guest gets only one cookie. Twelve divided by twelve is one.

6. Write down the five different division problems you just solved:

12 ÷ 2 = 6

12 ÷ 3 = 4

12 ÷ 4 = 3

12 ÷ 6 = 2

12 ÷ 12 = 1

If you had enough cookies and enough plates, you could solve any division problem no matter how large the numbers.

7. Now you and your friends can eat all the cookies.

3

Division as Repeated Subtraction

Another way to think of division is a method called "repeated subtraction." It is called repeated subtraction because you repeatedly subtract the divisor from the dividend until you get to 0 and have nothing left. The number of times you subtract the divisor from the dividend to get to 0 is the quotient. Try this activity to practice division as repeated subtraction.

MATERIALS

30 paper clips
pencil
paper

Procedure

1. The problem is 30 ÷ 10. Here's how you find the quotient with repeated subtraction. Start with thirty paper clips. Thirty is the dividend. Take away ten paper clips and put them in a pile. Ten is the divisor. Take away ten more paper clips and put them in a second pile. Take away the last ten paper clips and put them in a third pile. How many times did you subtract 10 from 30 to get to 0? Count the piles of paper clips you made. You should have three piles of ten paper clips, so 30 ÷ 10 = 3. Three is the quotient.

9

2. If you don't have paper clips handy, you can subtract 10's using pencil and paper instead.

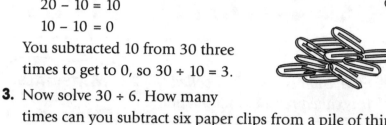

$$30 - 10 = 20$$
$$20 - 10 = 10$$
$$10 - 10 = 0$$

You subtracted 10 from 30 three times to get to 0, so $30 \div 10 = 3$.

3. Now solve $30 \div 6$. How many times can you subtract six paper clips from a pile of thirty? Put your thirty paper clips in one big pile. Then make piles of six paper clips until you have no paper clips left. How many piles did you make? Count them. There should be five piles of six paper clips, so $30 \div 6 = 5$. Five is the quotient. If you don't have paper clips, you can use pencil and paper to repeatedly subtract 6's.

4. What is $30 \div 2$? Put your thirty paper clips in one big pile again, then make piles of two paper clips until none are left. How many times did you subtract 2 from 30 to get to 0? You should have fifteen piles of two paper clips, so $30 \div 2 = 15$. Fifteen is the quotient.

You can use the repeated subtraction method to solve any division problem. Just subtract the divisor. When you get to 0, count the number of times you subtracted the given number and that's your answer.

1. What is $33 \div 11$?

Just keep subtracting the divisor from the dividend until you get to 0.

$33 - 11 = 22$

$22 - 11 = 11$

$11 - 11 = 0$

Since you subtracted 11 from 33 three times, $33 \div 11 = 3$.

2. What is $125 \div 25$?

$125 - 25 = 100$

$100 - 25 = 75$

$75 - 25 = 50$

$50 - 25 = 25$

$25 - 25 = 0$

You subtracted 25 from 125 five times, so $125 \div 25 = 5$.

Now see if you can solve these division problems using the subtraction method.

3. What is $60 \div 12$?

4. What is $90 \div 15$?

5. What is $162 \div 18$?

4

Division as the Opposite of Multiplication

There is a third way to understand and solve division problems. Just think of them as backward multiplication problems. In fact, division is often called the "inverse" (opposite) of multiplication.

MATERIALS

pencil
paper

Procedure

1. In multiplication, the two numbers that are multiplied are called "factors," and the answer is called the "product." In the multiplication problem

$3 \times 4 = 12$, the numbers

3 and 4 are the factors

and 12 is the product. To change this to a division problem, first read it backward starting with the product: $12 = 4 \times 3$. Then change the equals sign to a division sign and the multiplication sign to an equals sign: $12 \div 4 = 3$. The two problems are the opposite or the inverse of each other: $3 \times 4 = 12$ and $12 \div 4 = 3$. You can also swap the factors in the original multiplication problem to get $12 = 3 \times 4$ and $12 \div 3 = 4$.

$3 \times 4 = 12$

$12 \div 4 = 3$

2. Look at the multiplication problem $7 \times 7 = 49$. Write it backward: $49 = 7 \times 7$. Now change it to a division problem, $49 \div 7 = 7$. The two problems are the inverse of each other: $7 \times 7 = 49$ and $49 \div 7 = 7$. Both factors are the same, 7, so you can only change $7 \times 7 = 49$ into one division problem.

3. You can change any multiplication problem with two different factors into two division problems. Take the problem $72 \times 128 = 9,206$. You can write it backward as $9,206 = 128 \times 72$ or as $9,206 = 72 \times 128$. The two division problems become $9,206 = 128 = 72$ and $9,206 \div 72 = 128$.

4. Now that you understand the relationship between division and multiplication, you can use this relationship to solve a division problem. What is $18 \div 2$? Rewrite this as a multiplication problem. Oops! Something is missing. First write it as $18 \div 2 = $ *what?* Now rewrite this division problem

BRAIN Stretchers

Division is the opposite of multiplication in another way. Just as multiplication is repeated addition, division is repeated subtraction. For example, in the problem $30 \div 10 = 3$, the number 10 is subtracted three times from 30. Write this as a multiplication problem: $3 \times 10 = 30$. This means that 10 is added three times to get 30. You can use this handy method to find the missing factor in any division problem rewritten as a multiplication problem.

See if you can solve these division problems using the "opposite of multiplication" method.

1. What is $32 \div 4$?
2. What is $50 \div 5$?
3. What is $72 \div 9$?

as a multiplication problem. It becomes *what* × 2 =18? Can you figure out what factor the word *what* stands for? The answer is 9, because 9 × 2 = 18. Now change this problem back to a division problem: 18 ÷ 2 = 9. Nine is the quotient. It's easy to understand and solve division problems when you know that they are the opposite of multiplication problems.

~~~~ II ~~~~
UNDERSTANDING DIVISION FACTS

$\frac{36}{6}$

$24 \div 2 = 12$

$6\overline{)12}$

$18 \div 6 = 3$

$80\overline{)1500}$ 18R75

$9\overline{)1800}$

$4\overline{)32}$

$21 \div 7 = 3$

$70\overline{)490}$ 7

Now that you know what division is, you're ready to learn how to divide by 1, 2, 3, 4, 5, 6, 7, 8, 9, and 10. When you can divide by these ten numbers, you can solve any division problem. This section will introduce one hundred division facts using a variety of activities. Once you understand all the division facts, it won't take you long to commit them to memory.

5

Fun One!

Learn how to divide by 1 using a pile of books.

MATERIALS

10 books

Procedure

1. Stack all the books on a chair beside a table. Pretend there is one imaginary student working at the table. The student stands for the divisor, 1.

2. Put one of the books on the table and give it to the student. How many books did the student get? One book divided by one student is one book, so $1 \div 1 = 1$.

3. Put another book on the table and give the two books to the student. How many books did the student get? Two books divided by one student is two books, so $2 \div 1 = 2$.

4. Now put another book on the table and give all three books to the student. How many books did the student get? Three, so 3 ÷ 1 = 3.

5. Use the remaining seven books to divide by 1 and demonstrate the division-by-one facts.

Division by One

1 ÷ 1 = 1

2 ÷ 1 = 2

3 ÷ 1 = 3

4 ÷ 1 = 4

5 ÷ 1 = 5

6 ÷ 1 = 6

7 ÷ 1 = 7

8 ÷ 1 = 8

9 ÷ 1 = 9

10 ÷ 1 = 10

BRAIN Stretchers

Any number divided by 1 is itself.

53 ÷ 1 = 53

100 ÷ 1 = 100

2,345 ÷ 1 = 2,345

6,423,905 ÷ 1 = 6,423,905

1. What is 10 billion divided by 1?

2. What is 36 trillion divided by 1?

SUPER BRAIN Stretcher

The number 1 is called the "identity element" for division. This means that any number divided by 1 is that number. One is also the identity element for multiplication. Any number times 1 is that number.

Crazy Applications

- John's mother told him to share a box of thirty-six pencils with his friends. But John was alone. How many pencils did John get? What is 36 ÷ 1?

- If 117 cookies were served at a party with only one guest, how many cookies would that guest get? What is 117 ÷ 1?

It's All in the Eyes

With this activity, it won't take long for you to "see" the answers when dividing by 2.

Procedure

1. Page through magazines or catalogs and cut out ten pairs of eyes from pictures of faces. Cut each pair of eyes in half so that you have twenty individual eyes. Place all twenty eyes on a piece of paper.

2. Take two of the eyes and place them in front of you on a table. Group the eyes in a pair, as if they were on a face. How many pairs of eyes do you have? You should have one pair. You just demonstrated the first division-by-two fact: 2 ÷ 2 = 1. Put the eyes back on the piece of paper.

3. Take four eyes and group them in pairs. You should have enough pairs of eyes for two faces, so 4 ÷ 2 = 2.

4. How many pairs of eyes can you make with six eyes? Divide six eyes into pairs. You should have three pairs, so 6 ÷ 2 = 3.

5. Use this method to demonstrate the rest of the division-by-two facts.

BRAIN Stretcher

Notice that all the dividends in the division-by-two problems are even numbers. Any even number divided by 2 will give you a whole number. Any odd number divided by 2 will give you a whole number and a fraction.

Division by Two
2 ÷ 2 = 1
4 ÷ 2 = 2
6 ÷ 2 = 3
8 ÷ 2 = 4
10 ÷ 2 = 5
12 ÷ 2 = 6
14 ÷ 2 = 7
16 ÷ 2 = 8
18 ÷ 2 = 9
20 ÷ 2 = 10

Crazy Applications

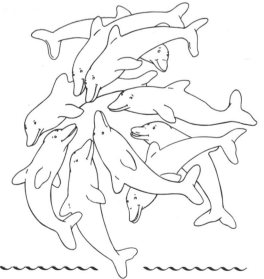

▼ Four socks are in the bottom of a drawer. How many pairs of socks are there? What is 4 ÷ 2?

▼ Sixteen wheels on bikes just zipped by. How many bikes are there? What is 16 ÷ 2?

▼ Twenty dolphin eyes peek from the water. How many dolphins are there? What is 20 ÷ 2?

Division Circles

Use a jar of pennies to help you learn to divide by 3.

MATERIALS

pencil
paper
jar of 30
pennies

Procedure

1. At the top of a piece of paper, write "Division-by-Three Problems." Draw three large circles on the paper. Number the circles from 1 to 3. Your paper should look like the one here.

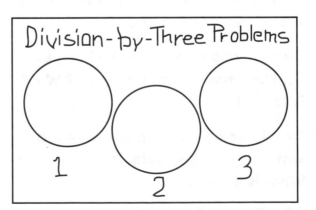

2. Take three pennies from the jar and put a penny in each circle. How many pennies are in each circle? One, so 3 ÷ 3 = 1.

3. Put a second penny in each of the three circles. How many pennies did you use altogether? Six. How many pennies are in each circle? Two, so 6 ÷ 3 = 2.

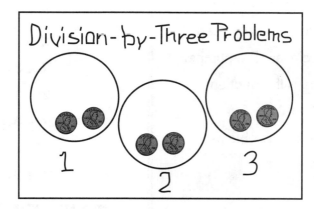

4. Take three more pennies from the jar and put a penny in each circle. How many pennies did you use altogether? Nine. How many pennies are in each circle now? Three, so 9 ÷ 3 = 3.

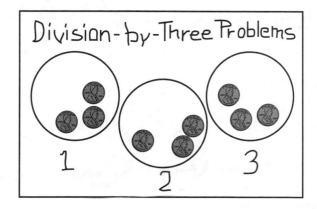

5. Use this method with the rest of the pennies to demonstrate the remaining division-by-three facts.

Y ou can use the penny system to solve any division problem. If the problem was 18 ÷ 6, you would draw six circles on a piece of paper and distribute eighteen pennies among the six circles. The number of pennies in each circle is the quotient. So 18 ÷ 6 = 3.

Try to solve these division problems using the penny system:

1. What is 45 ÷ 5?

2. What is 100 ÷ 4?

3. What is 32 ÷ 8?

Division by Three
3 ÷ 3 = 1
6 ÷ 3 = 2
9 ÷ 3 = 3
12 ÷ 3 = 4
15 ÷ 3 = 5
18 ÷ 3 = 6
21 ÷ 3 = 7
24 ÷ 3 = 8
27 ÷ 3 = 9
30 ÷ 3 = 10

Crazy Applications

• **Nine wheels on tricycles roll down the sidewalk. How many tricycles are there? What is 9 ÷ 3?**

• **Fifteen legs hold up a group of three-legged stools. How many stools are there? What is 15 ÷ 3?**

Number Line Fours

You can use a number line to divide by 4.

MATERIALS

pencil
paper

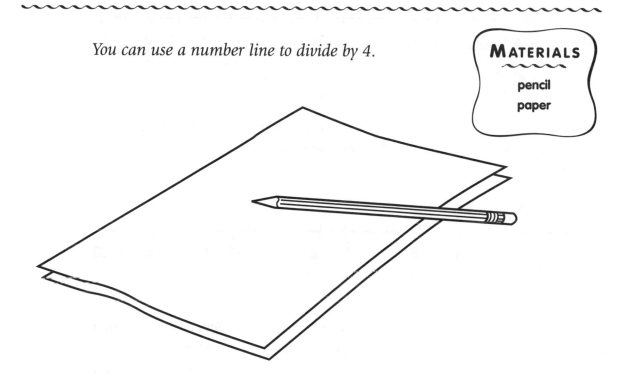

Procedure

1. Write the numbers from 0 to 20 on a number line as shown.

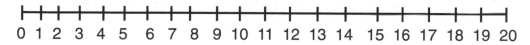

0 1 2 3 4 5 6 7 8 9 10 11 12 13 14 15 16 17 18 19 20

2. To use this number line to solve 4 ÷ 4, first put your pencil on the 4.

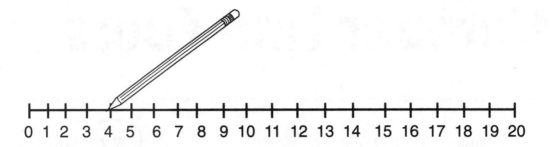

3. Next count backward four spaces and draw an arc to this number. You should have landed on 0. How many arcs did you draw? One, so 4 ÷ 4 = 1.

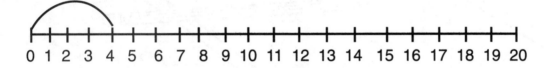

4. Now use a new number line to solve 8 ÷ 4. Put your pencil on the 8, then count backward four spaces and draw an arc to the number 4. Count backward four more spaces and draw an arc to the 0. How many arcs did you draw? Two, so 8 ÷ 4 = 2.

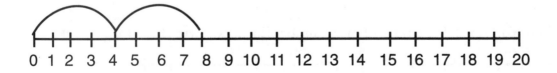

5. Now use a new number line to solve 12 ÷ 4. Put your pencil on the number 12 and count backward four spaces. Draw an arc from 12 to 8. Count backward four more spaces and draw an arc from 8 to 4. Count backward four more spaces and draw an arc from 4 to 0. Now count the arcs you have drawn. You drew three arcs, so 12 ÷ 4 = 3.

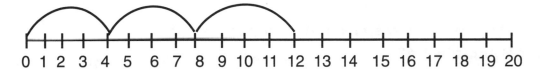

6. Use this method with a number line forty spaces long to demonstrate the remaining division-by-four facts.

Division by Four

4 ÷ 4 = 1

8 ÷ 4 = 2

12 ÷ 4 = 3

16 ÷ 4 = 4

20 ÷ 4 = 5

24 ÷ 4 = 6

28 ÷ 4 = 7

32 ÷ 4 = 8

36 ÷ 4 = 9

40 ÷ 4 = 10

BRAIN Stretchers

1. You can use a number line to solve any division problem. Solve 8 ÷ 2 on a number line. Check your answer by looking at the Division-by-Two table in chapter 6.

2. Solve 15 ÷ 3 using a number line. How many arcs did you draw? Check your answer by looking at the Division-by-Three table in chapter 7.

If you had a long enough number line and enough patience, you could use this method to solve 122 ÷ 2, 57 ÷ 3, or 96 ÷ 4!

Crazy Applications

- Eight zebra legs trotted by. How many zebras are there? What is 8 ÷ 4?

- Sixteen wheels whizzed by. How many cars went by? What is 16 ÷ 4?

- Thirty-two chair legs were around a table. How many chairs were there? What is 32 ÷ 4?

Nickel Mania

Dividing by 5 is as easy as making change.
All you have to do is follow these simple steps.

Procedure

1. Think of 5 as 5¢, which is five pennies or a nickel. Exchange five pennies for an equal value of nickels. How many nickels do you have? One, so 5 ÷ 5 = 1.

2. Try this problem: What is 10 ÷ 5? Think of 10 as 10¢ or a dime. Exchange the dime for an equal value of nickels. How many nickels do you have? Two, so 10 ÷ 5 = 2.

3. What is 15 ÷ 5? Use a dime and five pennies, or 15¢, to represent 15. Exchange them for an equal value of nickels. How many nickels do you have? Three, so 15 ÷ 5 = 3.

4. What is 20 ÷ 5? Use two dimes, or 20¢, to represent 20. Exchange each dime for two nickels. How many nickels do you have? Four, so 20 ÷ 5 = 4.

5. What is 25 ÷ 5? Think of 25 as 25¢ or a quarter. Exchange the quarter for an equal value of nickels. How many nickels do you have? Five, so 25 ÷ 5 = 5.

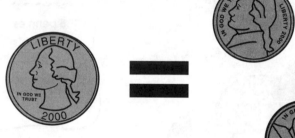

Division by Five
5 ÷ 5 = 1
10 ÷ 5 = 2
15 ÷ 5 = 3
20 ÷ 5 = 4
25 ÷ 5 = 5
30 ÷ 5 = 6
35 ÷ 5 = 7
40 ÷ 5 = 8
45 ÷ 5 = 9
50 ÷ 5 = 10

6. Use the nickel method to demonstrate the other division-by-five facts.

You can use the nickel method to divide any number by 5. What is 90 ÷ 5? Use three quarters, a dime, and five pennies to represent 90. Exchange each quarter for five nickels, the dime for two nickels, and the pennies for one nickel. Count how many nickels you have altogether. You have 18 nickels, so 90 ÷ 5 = 18.

Now see if you can solve these problems. Use your coins.

1. What is 65 ÷ 5?

2. What is 95 ÷ 5?

3. What is 110 ÷ 5?

4. What is 200 ÷ 5?

Crazy Applications

▼ Ten fingers are typing. How many hands are typing? What is 10 ÷ 5?

▼ Twenty toes are standing in the ocean. How many feet are there? What is 20 ÷ 5?

▼ Thirty-five starfish arms are sitting at the bottom of the ocean. How many starfish are there? What is 35 ÷ 5?

Subtracting Sixes

You can divide by 6 using egg cartons.

MATERIALS

5 empty egg
cartons

60 marbles

Procedure

1. Break the egg cartons in half. Each half carton has six compartments, so it represents the divisor 6. The marbles are the dividend.

2. What is 6 ÷ 6? Count out six marbles. Put one marble in each section of a half carton. How many half cartons do the six marbles fill? One, so 6 ÷ 6 = 1.

3. What is 6 ÷ 2? Put the marbles back and count out twelve marbles. Use the twelve marbles to fill the half cartons. How many half cartons do the twelve marbles fill? Two, so 12 ÷ 6 = 2.

4. What is 18 ÷ 6? Put the marbles back and use eighteen marbles to fill the half cartons. How many half cartons did you fill? Three, so 18 ÷ 6 = 3.

5. Use the half-carton method to demonstrate the rest of the division-by-six facts.

Division by Six

$$6 \div 6 = 1$$
$$12 \div 6 = 2$$
$$18 \div 6 = 3$$
$$24 \div 6 = 4$$
$$30 \div 6 = 5$$
$$36 \div 6 = 6$$
$$42 \div 6 = 7$$
$$48 \div 6 = 8$$
$$54 \div 6 = 9$$
$$60 \div 6 = 10$$

BRAIN Stretcher

You can use the half-carton method to divide by 6 no matter how large the dividend. What is $72 \div 6$? Just collect enough egg cartons and break them in half, or reuse one half carton and keep a record of how many times you can fill it with marbles.

Crazy Applications

● If every stop sign has six corners, how many stop signs have a total of eighteen corners? What is $18 \div 6$?

● If fifty-four ant legs march toward a picnic, how many ants are there? What is $54 \div 6$?

Calculating Sevens

You can use a calculator to divide by 7.

MATERIALS

calculator

Procedure

1. See if you can find the dividends that
when divided by 7 will give the
quotients 1, 2, 3, 4, 5, 6, 7, 8, 9,
and 10. Start by trying to find
the quotient 1. Enter
the following
problems
into the calculator
until you get the
answer 1.

$1 \div 7 =$
$2 \div 7 =$
$3 \div 7 =$
$4 \div 7 =$
$5 \div 7 =$
$6 \div 7 =$
$7 \div 7 =$
$8 \div 7 =$

Was the answer to any of these problems 1? You found the first division-
by-seven fact: $7 \div 7 = 1$.

2. Now keep dividing by 7 until you find the dividend that when divided by 7 has the quotient 2. This time start with 11.

$11 \div 7 =$

$12 \div 7 =$

$13 \div 7 =$

$14 \div 7 =$

$15 \div 7 =$

Is the answer to any of these problems 2? Yes. So $14 \div 7 = 2$.

3. Now see if you can find a dividend that has the quotient 3.

4. Use this method with your calculator to demonstrate the remaining division-by-seven facts.

Division by Seven

$7 \div 7 = 1$

$14 \div 7 = 2$

$21 \div 7 = 3$

$28 \div 7 = 4$

$35 \div 7 = 5$

$42 \div 7 = 6$

$49 \div 7 = 7$

$56 \div 7 = 8$

$63 \div 7 = 9$

$70 \div 7 = 10$

BRAIN Stretcher

You can use a calculator to solve any division problem. Sometimes when you solve a division problem on a calculator, a decimal point pops up. A decimal point looks like a period (.). A decimal point means the dividend did not divide evenly. For example, $12 \div 6 = 2$, but if you divide 15 by 6, the calculator will give the quotient 2.5, which is read as two point five, or two and one-half. When the calculator tried to divide 15 by 6, it could not divide evenly. The calculator divided the leftover number by the divisor, which produced the decimal fraction.

Crazy Applications

▼ How many weeks until your birthday if it is 35 days away?
What is 35 ÷ 7?

▼ If you have eight pizzas, how many slices do you need to
cut each pizza into to have fifty-six slices altogether?
What is 56 ÷ 8?

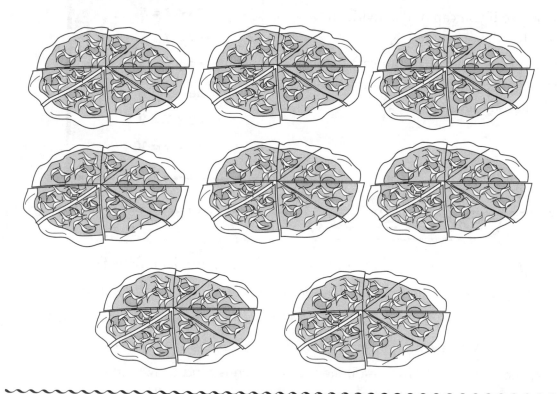

Opposite Eights

Division is always easier when you already know your multiplication tables. Try this activity to see how easy it can be. If you know how to multiply by 8, you can automatically divide by 8.

MATERIALS

pencil
paper

Procedure

1. Start with the problem 8 ÷ 8. First, write this division problem as a multiplication problem: 8 = 8 × *what?* The dividend (8) is the product of the multiplication problem, and the divisor (8) is one of the factors. The other factor (*what?*) is missing. If you know your multiplication tables, then you know 1 × 8 = 8. Since 1 is the missing factor, 8 ÷ 8 = 1.

2. What is 16 ÷ 8? Change this division problem into a multiplication problem with a missing factor to solve it: 16 = 8 × *what?* Since 2 × 8 = 16, the missing factor is 2. So 16 ÷ 8 = 2.

3. What is $24 \div 8$? Rewrite the problem as $24 = 8 \times$ *what?* Since $3 \times 8 = 24$, $24 \div 8 = 3$.

4. Use the 8 times table to demonstrate the rest of the division-by-eight facts. If you don't remember all of your 8 times table, use these multiplication facts to write each division problem as a multiplication problem: $1 \times 8 = 8$, $2 \times 8 = 16$, $3 \times 8 = 24$, $4 \times 8 = 32$, $5 \times 8 = 40$, $6 \times 8 = 48$, $7 \times 8 = 56$, $8 \times 8 = 64$, $9 \times 8 = 72$, $10 \times 8 = 80$.

Division by Eight
$8 \div 8 = 1$
$16 \div 8 = 2$
$24 \div 8 = 3$
$32 \div 8 = 4$
$40 \div 8 = 5$
$48 \div 8 = 6$
$56 \div 8 = 7$
$64 \div 8 = 8$
$72 \div 8 = 9$
$80 \div 8 = 10$

BRAIN Stretcher

Here's how the parts of a division problem and a multiplication problem fit together. Take the division problem $48 \div 8 = 6$, which is the opposite of the multiplication problem $6 \times 8 = 48$.

- The dividend of the division problem is the product of the multiplication problem (48).
- The divisor of the division problem is one of the factors of the multiplication problem (8).
- The quotient of the division problem is the other factor of the multiplication problem (6). The problems fit together like this:

quotient x divisor = dividend

product ÷ factor = factor

Crazy Applications

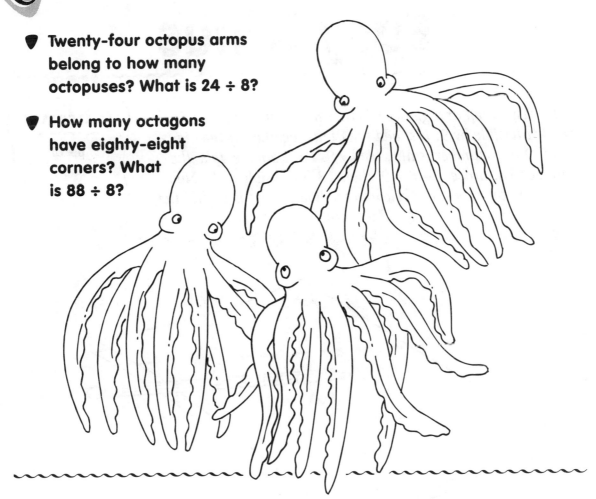

- Twenty-four octopus arms belong to how many octopuses? What is 24 ÷ 8?

- How many octagons have eighty-eight corners? What is 88 ÷ 8?

Nice and Easy Nines

It's easy to tell at a glance whether a two-digit number is evenly divisible by 9. Just add the digits together. If the digits total 9, the number is divisible by 9. For example, take the number 18. Since 1 + 8 = 9, then 18 is divisible by 9. Now just follow the procedure below to see how easy it is to find the answers to two-digit division-by-nine problems.

MATERIALS

pencil

paper

Procedure

1. Once you determine that a two-digit number is divisible by 9, here's how to find the quotient of the problem. Just add 1 to the digit in the tens place. For example, take the problem 18 ÷ 9. First determine if 18 is

divisible by 9. Add 1 + 8. The answer is 9, so 18 is divisible by 9. What number is in the tens place? It's 1. Add 1 to the 1 in the tens place: 1 + 1 = 2. So 18 ÷ 9 = 2. Amazing!

2. Try 27 ÷ 9. First determine if 27 is divisible by 9. Add 2 + 7. The answer is 9, so 27 is divisible by 9. Now add 1 to the 2 in the tens place: 2 + 1 = 3. So 27 ÷ 9 = 3. Incredible!

3. What is 36 ÷ 9? First determine if 36 is divisible by 9. Add 3 + 6. The answer is 9, so 36 is divisible by 9. Now add 1 to the 3 in the tens place: 3 + 1 = 4. So 36 ÷ 9 = 4. Wow!

4. Use this method to demonstrate the rest of the division-by-nine facts.

Division by Nine
9 ÷ 9 = 1
18 ÷ 9 = 2
27 ÷ 9 = 3
36 ÷ 9 = 4
45 ÷ 9 = 5
54 ÷ 9 = 6
63 ÷ 9 = 7
72 ÷ 9 = 8
81 ÷ 9 = 9
90 ÷ 9 = 10

BRAIN Stretchers

How can you tell if a three-digit number is divisible by 9? Just add all three digits. If they add up to 9, then the number is divisible by 9!

1. Is 135 divisible by 9? Yes, because 1 + 3 + 5 = 9.

2. Is 873 divisible by 9? First add all three digits: 8 + 7 + 3 = 18. Now add the digits in the answer: 1 + 8 = 9. So 873 is divisible by 9!

3. Which of the following numbers are divisible by 9?

102	207
360	422
579	819

Crazy Applications

- Thirty-six children showed up to play baseball. Nine players were placed on each team. How many teams were formed? What is 36 ÷ 9?

- A teacher had a basket that contained forty-five strawberries. She wanted to divide them equally among nine students. How many strawberries did each student get? What is 45 ÷ 9?

- A girl had a box of eighty-one dog biscuits. She wanted to divide them equally among nine Irish setter puppies. How many biscuits did each puppy get? What is 81 ÷ 9?

Erasing Zeros

Dividing by 10 is easy. All you have to do is erase one 0 from the dividend!

MATERIALS

pencil
paper
eraser

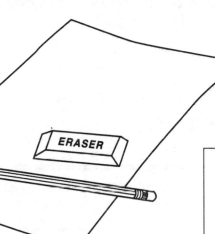

ERASER

Procedure

1. What is 10 ÷ 10? Write the dividend (10) on a piece of paper. There is only one zero. Erase it. What's left? The 1, so 10 ÷ 10 = 1.

2. What is 20 ÷ 10? Write 20 on a piece of paper, then erase the 0. What's left? The 2, so 20 ÷ 10 = 2.

3. What is 30 ÷ 10? Write 30, then erase the 0. What's left? Just the 3, so 30 ÷ 10 = 3.

4. Use the erasing-zeros method to demonstrate the rest of the division-by-ten facts.

Division by Ten
10 ÷ 10 = 1
20 ÷ 10 = 2
30 ÷ 10 = 3
40 ÷ 10 = 4
50 ÷ 10 = 5
60 ÷ 10 = 6
70 ÷ 10 = 7
80 ÷ 10 = 8
90 ÷ 10 = 9
100 ÷ 10 = 10

You can use the erasing-zeros method to divide any number that is divisible by ten. (An easy way to tell if a number is divisible by 10 is if it has a 0 on the end. If it does, it is!) What is $140 \div 10$? Just erase one 0 from the dividend (140). So $140 \div 10 = 14$. What is $3,200 \div 10$? Erase one 0 from 3,200. So $3,200 \div 10 = 320$.

Use the "erase one zero" rule to solve the following division problems:

1. What is $350 \div 10$?

2. What is $700 \div 10$?

3. What is $1,020 \div 10$?

4. What is $5,000,000 \div 10$?

Crazy Applications

- Forty bowling pins were standing upright ready for players. How many sets of pins were there? What is $40 \div 10$?

- How many dimes could you make from seventy pennies? What is $70 \div 10$?

- How many children in a family if the children have ninety fingers altogether? What is $90 \div 10$?

It's just as easy to divide by 100 as it is to divide by 10. To divide by 100, just erase two 0's from the dividend.

$$500 \div 100 = 5$$
$$7,000 \div 100 = 70$$

Now see if you can do these problems:

1. What is $600 \div 100$?

2. What is $9,000 \div 100$?

3. What is $10,400 \div 100$?

4. What is $3,000,000 \div 100$?

How do you think you divide by 1,000? You're right. Just erase three 0's!

Dividing by Zero

Wondering how to divide by 0? The answer is you can't. Ever. Try this activity to see why.

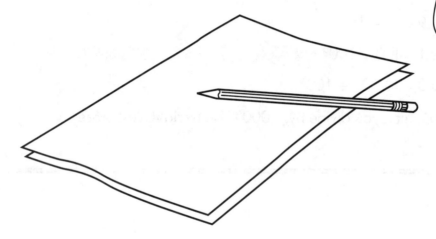

Procedure

1. As you saw in chapter 3, repeated subtraction is one way to solve a division problem. You keep subtracting the divisor from the dividend until you get to 0. Once you get to 0, you count how many times you subtracted the divisor, and that's the quotient. What would happen if you tried to use this method to figure out the problem 5 ÷ 0? You want to subtract 0 from 5 until you get to 0, then count how many times you subtracted 0. That's your answer. So subtract 0: 5 − 0 = 5.

2. Now subtract 0 again: 5 − 0 = 5.

3. And again: 5 − 0 = 5.

4. Did you get to 0? No. No matter how many times you subtract 0, you're going to end up with 5. You'll never get to 0. For this reason, you cannot divide by 0. Division by 0 is undefined. No matter what number you divide by 0, the answer is always undefined.

5. You should have no problem demonstrating the division-by-zero facts.

Division by Zero

$1 \div 0 =$ **undefined**

$2 \div 0 =$ **undefined**

$3 \div 0 =$ **undefined**

$4 \div 0 =$ **undefined**

$5 \div 0 =$ **undefined**

$6 \div 0 =$ **undefined**

$7 \div 0 =$ **undefined**

$8 \div 0 =$ **undefined**

$9 \div 0 =$ **undefined**

$10 \div 0 =$ **undefined**

BRAIN Stretchers

1. What is $100 \div 0$? It's undefined!

2. What is $531/0$? Undefined!

3. What is $0\overline{)1,234,567}$? Undefined!

4. Now can you answer these problems?

63/0

111/0

Another way to understand that division by 0 is undefined is to think of division as the opposite of multiplication. If 6 ÷ 3 = 2, then 2 × 3 = 6.

In a division problem, the quotient times the divisor always equals the dividend. To find the quotient of 10 ÷ 2, all you have to do is answer the question, What number times 2 (the divisor) will give you 10 (the dividend)? Five. Since 5 × 2 = 10, then 10 ÷ 2 = 5.

Now try to solve the problem 10 ÷ 0. What number times 0 will give you 10? There is no such number. Any number times 0 is always 0. That is why division by 0 is undefined.

~~~ III ~~~

DIVISION PRACTICE GAMES

The activities in this section will help you learn the one hundred basic division facts in fun and creative ways. Play a game of tic-tac-toe that challenges you to know a division fact before you can place your X or O. Play a popular memory game—using division facts, of course. Or search for division problems in a division search the way you would search for words in a word search. Some of the games require speed as well as accuracy, others just accuracy. The one thing they all have in common is that they are fun and will teach you the one hundred basic division facts. The more you play these games, the more you'll learn.

Division Tic-Tac-Toe

Play this simple game of tic-tac-toe with a friend while you practice dividing by 2, 5, and 10.

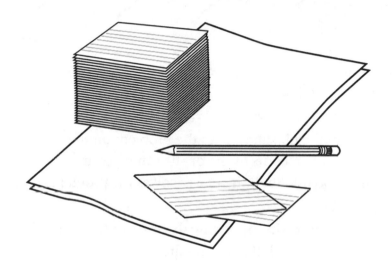

MATERIALS

pencil
several pieces
of paper
30 index cards
2 players

Game Preparation

Write one of the following division problems on each of the thirty index cards:

2 ÷ 2	12 ÷ 2	5 ÷ 5	30 ÷ 5	10 ÷ 10	60 ÷ 10
4 ÷ 2	14 ÷ 2	10 ÷ 5	35 ÷ 5	20 ÷ 10	70 ÷ 10
6 ÷ 2	16 ÷ 2	15 ÷ 5	40 ÷ 5	30 ÷ 10	80 ÷ 10
8 ÷ 2	18 ÷ 2	20 ÷ 5	45 ÷ 5	40 ÷ 10	90 ÷ 10
10 ÷ 2	20 ÷ 2	25 ÷ 5	50 ÷ 5	50 ÷ 10	100 ÷ 10

Game Rules

1. Draw a tic-tac-toe board on a piece of paper.

2. Shuffle the index cards and place them facedown in the center of the table.

3. Player 1 draws a card from the pile and solves the division problem written on it. For example, if the problem is 8 ÷ 2, the correct answer is 4. If player 1 solves the problem correctly by saying, "Four," he or she can place an X anywhere on the tic-tac-toe board. But if the player solves the problem incorrectly, he or she loses that turn.

4. Player 2 then draws a card from the pile and solves the problem on the card. If the player solves the problem correctly, he or she can place an O in any remaining space on the board. But if the player solves the problem incorrectly, he or she loses that turn.

5. The game continues until one player wins by getting three X's or O's in a row, or no one gets three in a row and all the squares are filled.

6. Start another Division Tic-Tac-Toe game, using the same rules. When there are no cards left, the player who has won the most games is the winner.

Split Second

In this game, you compete against your friends and test the speed and accuracy with which you can solve division problems.

MATERIALS

pencil
several pieces
of paper
dice
timer or clock
with second hand
2 players

Game Rules

1. On a piece of paper, player 2 writes down five problems from the division tables for player 1 to solve.

2. Player 1 rolls the dice and multiplies the numbers rolled to determine how many seconds he or she has to solve all of the problems. Remember, multiplication is repeated addition. If player 1 rolls a 3 and a 5, either add 3 five times or add 5 three times to get 15. Player 1 would have 15 seconds to solve the problems.

3. Player 2 places the problems facedown in front of player 1. When player 1 turns the problems faceup, player 2 sets the timer. Player 1 solves as many of the problems as he or she can before the time is up and player 2 shouts, "Stop!" Player 1 earns 1 point for each problem solved correctly.

4. The players switch roles and play again.

5. The first player to earn 21 points is the winner.

Division Search

In this game, two or more players search for division problems and their answers in a number puzzle.

MATERIALS

several pencils
several pieces of
graph paper
2 or more
players

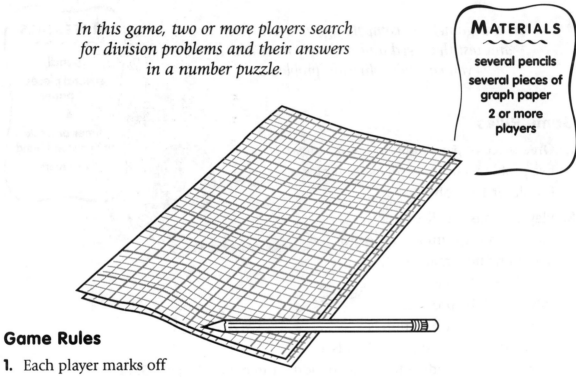

Game Rules

1. Each player marks off an area that is seven squares by seven squares on his or her piece of graph paper.

2. In these forty-nine squares, each player makes a number puzzle by hiding ten division problems and their answers. The problems can be hidden horizontally or vertically. The numbers should be one or two digits. Use two adjacent squares for two-digit numbers. Fill in the unused spaces with random numbers.

3. The players switch puzzles. The first player to find all ten hidden problems is the winner.

Here is a sample Division Search puzzle. Ten problems and their answers are hidden. Can you find them?

1	0	5	2	2	1	1
9	3	4	6	8	4	2
5	3	9	4	5	2	1
8	0	7	8	8	7	2
1	6	7	8	3	9	4
3	5	4	6	3	3	3
7	7	1	2	9	0	6

1	0	5	2	2	1	1
9	3	4	6	8	4	2
5	3	9	4	5	2	1
8	0	7	8	8	7	2
1	6	7	8	3	9	4
3	5	4	6	3	3	3
7	7	1	2	9	0	6

Look in the first row at the first four numbers: 1, 0, 5, 2. You have found the first hidden division problem: $10 \div 5 = 2$.

1	0	5	2	2	1	1
9	3	4	6	8	4	2
5	3	9	4	5	2	1
8	0	7	8	8	7	2
1	6	7	8	3	9	4
3	5	4	6	3	3	3
7	7	1	2	9	0	6

Now look in the second column. The third to sixth numbers are 3, 0, 6, 5. You have found the second hidden problem: $30 \div 6 = 5$.

Now find the other eight hidden problems.

SUPER DIVISION SEARCH

Mark off a ten-by-ten grid. Hide ten multiplication and ten division
problems in the grid.

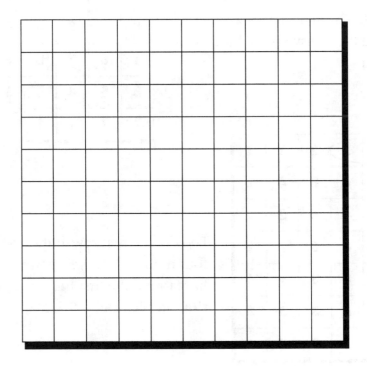

Off to the Races

In this speedy contest, two or more players compete to see who can say division facts the fastest.

Game Preparation

At the top of a blackboard, write "Record Holders." Down the left-hand side of the board, write the numbers 1 to 10 followed by a division sign (÷) as shown.

Game Rules

1. Player 1 chooses a set of division facts to recite, such as the division-by-three facts. Player 2 times how fast the first player recites the entire set of division facts.

RECORD HOLDERS

1 ÷
2 ÷
3 ÷
4 ÷
5 ÷
6 ÷
7 ÷
8 ÷
9 ÷
10 ÷

2. Player 1 starts out as the record holder. His or her name and time are recorded on the Record Holders board next to the division facts chosen.

3. The other players in turn each recite a set of division facts. It can be the same set or a different one.

4. Any time a player sets a new record, the new record is written on the Record Holders board. Previous records are crossed out or erased.

5. The game can continue forever. Players can play any time they have a few extra minutes to try to beat the existing records. Keep the Record Holders board posted at all times.

OFF TO THE RACES SOLITAIRE

If you can't find a friend to practice with, compete against yourself. Write your times on the Record Holders board. Keep practicing, and as your times improve, erase your old times and put your new times on the board.

Division Memory

*Play this memory game with one or more friends
to help you remember the division facts.*

MATERIALS

pencil
80 index cards
calculator
2 or more
players

Game Preparation

1. Take forty index cards and write "DP" on one side of each.
DP stands for division problem. It tells you
that the card has a division problem on the
other side.

2. Take another forty index cards and write "A"
on one side of each. A stands for answer. It
tells you that the card has an answer on the
other side.

3. On the blank side of each DP card, write one
of the following division problems. These are
the problems most people have trouble remembering.

$8 \div 4$	$12 \div 6$	$14 \div 7$	$16 \div 8$	$18 \div 9$
$12 \div 4$	$18 \div 6$	$21 \div 7$	$24 \div 8$	$27 \div 9$
$16 \div 4$	$24 \div 6$	$28 \div 7$	$32 \div 8$	$36 \div 9$
$20 \div 4$	$30 \div 6$	$35 \div 7$	$40 \div 8$	$45 \div 9$
$24 \div 4$	$36 \div 6$	$42 \div 7$	$48 \div 8$	$54 \div 9$
$28 \div 4$	$42 \div 6$	$49 \div 7$	$56 \div 8$	$63 \div 9$
$32 \div 4$	$48 \div 6$	$56 \div 7$	$64 \div 8$	$72 \div 9$
$36 \div 4$	$54 \div 6$	$63 \div 7$	$72 \div 8$	$81 \div 9$

4. Write a 2 on the blank side of five A cards. Do the same for the numbers 3 to 9, so that there are five cards of each number.

5. Keep the DP cards and the A cards in two separate piles.

Game Rules

1. Shuffle the DP cards. Place them on the table in five rows, eight cards per row, so that the problem side of each card is facedown.

2. Shuffle all the A cards. Place them on the table in five rows so that the answer side of each card is facedown.

3. Players take turns turning over two cards, one DP card and one A card. If the card with the problem matches the card with the answer (cards match when the answer is correct), the player keeps the pair of cards and takes another turn. If the cards do not match (the answer is not a correct solution), then the cards are returned facedown to their original places and the next player takes a turn. (Use a calculator to check the answers to problems you're not sure about.)

4. Play continues until there are no cards left. The player with the most cards wins.

21 Three-in-a-Row Bingo

Practice your division facts and see
if you can get three in a row.

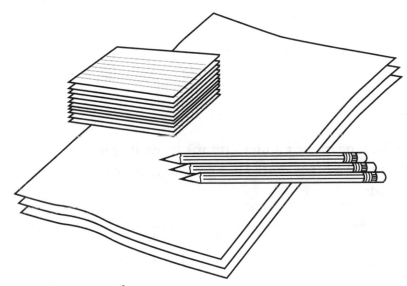

MATERIALS

several pencils

10 index cards

several pieces
of paper

2 or more
players

Game Preparation

Write a set of division facts without the answers on ten index cards, one
problem per card. For example, if you want to practice the division-by-seven
facts, you would write the following problems:

7 ÷ 7	14 ÷ 7	21 ÷ 7	28 ÷ 7	35 ÷ 7
42 ÷ 7	49 ÷ 7	56 ÷ 7	63 ÷ 7	70 ÷ 7

Game Rules

1. Each player makes his or her own Three-in-a-Row Bingo game card by drawing a large square on a piece of paper. Then draw two horizontal lines and two vertical lines in the square to make nine smaller squares as shown.

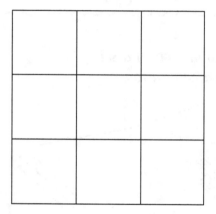

2. In the small squares, write nine of the numbers from 1 to 10. Players may arrange the numbers in any order they wish. Here are two examples of Three-in-a-Row Bingo cards.

6	4	3		2	5	6
5	8	9		3	1	10
7	10	2		8	7	9

3. Shuffle the cards and place them facedown in the center of the table.

4. Player 1 turns the top card over and solves the problem. If the answer matches a number on the player's bingo card, he or she marks an X through the number.

5. Player 2 takes a turn with the next card.

6. The first player to cross through three numbers in a row—either horizontally, vertically, or diagonally—wins the round.

7. For each new round, each player draws a new bingo card, placing the numbers in new places. Shuffle the cards and place them facedown. The first player to win three rounds wins the game.

FOUR-IN-A-ROW BINGO

Write a set of division problems on sixteen index cards that have the answers 1, 2, 3, 4, 5, 6, 7, 8, 9, 10, 11, 12, 20, 25, 50, and 100. Make bingo game cards that contain sixteen small squares, four across and four down. Players arrange the answers on their bingo cards in any order they wish. Play is the same as for Three-in-a-Row Bingo, except players try to cross through four numbers in a row.

22

Egg Carton Division

Use an egg carton to study simple division facts.

Procedure

1. Cut off the last two egg compartments so that the egg carton has space for only ten eggs.

2. Roll the dice. Combine the numbers on the dice to make two two-digit numbers. For example, if you roll a 3 and a 5, the two numbers would be 35 and 53.

3. Pick one of the two numbers. Is it divisible by any number from 2 to 10? Check and see. For example, if you think the number is divisible by 3, take as many marbles as the number you want to divide and distribute them equally among three of the egg compartments. If there are no marbles left over, the number is divisible by 3. Try this for the other number. What other numbers are your two numbers divisible by?

4. Roll the dice again and make another pair of numbers to practice egg carton division.

Answer Up!

Practice division facts by recalling their answers.

MATERIALS

pencil
30 index cards
die
several pieces
of paper
timer or watch
with second hand
2 or more
players

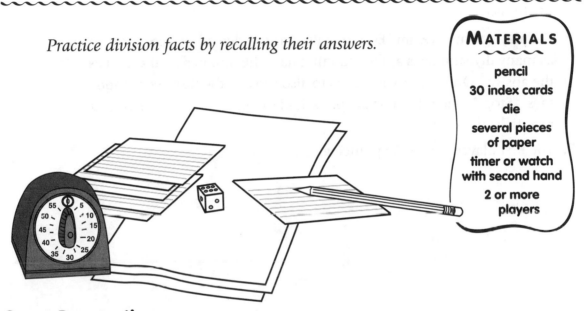

Game Preparation

1. Write the number 1 on two index cards. Do the same for the numbers 2 to 10, so that there are twenty cards altogether.

2. Write the words "Everyone Play" on ten other index cards. Below that, write one of the numbers from 1 to 10 on each of these cards.

Game Rules

1. Shuffle all the cards and place them facedown in one pile on the table.

2. Each player rolls the die. The player who rolls the highest number goes first.

3. Player 1 turns the top card over and on a piece of paper writes as many division facts as he or she can that have the number on the card as the answer. At the end of 1 minute, player 2, serving as the timekeeper, says, "Stop."

4. Player 1 is awarded 1 point for each correct division fact that has the turned-over number as the answer.

5. Player 2 turns the next card over and takes a turn while player 1 serves as the timekeeper.

6. If a player turns over an "Everyone Play" card, then all players write down as many division facts as they can that have the number on the card as the answer. One player volunteers to also serve as the timekeeper and says, "Stop." when the time is up. Each player earns 1 point for each correct division fact.

7. The first player to earn 50 points wins the game.

Mystery Number

Learn your division facts while guessing a mystery number.

MATERIALS

pencil

10 index cards

several small
pieces of paper

2 players

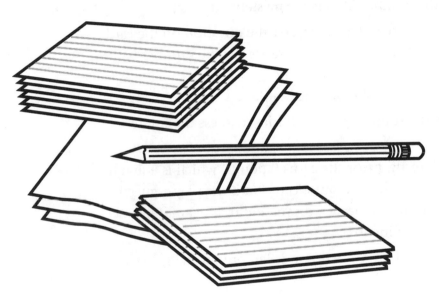

Game Preparation

Write one of the following questions on each of ten index cards:

Is the number larger than ____?

Is the number smaller than ____?

Is the number larger than ____?

Is the number smaller than ____?

Is the number divisible by 2?

Is the number divisible by 3?

Is the number divisible by 4?

Is the number divisible by 5?

Is the number divisible by 7?

Is the number divisible by 10?

Game Rules

1. Shuffle the cards and place them facedown in the center of the table.

2. Player 1 writes a number from 1 to 100 on a small piece of paper without letting player 2 see the number. This is the mystery number.

3. Player 2 draws the top card and asks player 1 the question on the card about the mystery number. If the question reads, "Is the number larger than _____?" or "Is the number smaller than _____?" player 2 can substitute any number he or she wishes for the blank.

4. Player 1 answers the question and player 2 tries to guess the mystery number.

5. If player 2 guesses correctly, he or she earns 9 points, which is equal to the number of remaining unasked questions. But if the player guesses incorrectly, he or she turns the next card over and tries again. Player 2 earns 1 less point for each incorrect guess.

6. The round continues until there are no cards left or player 2 guesses correctly.

7. Shuffle the cards and place them facedown again. This time player 2 writes a mystery number and player 1 tries to guess.

8. Play continues until one player earns 25 points.

SUPER MYSTERY NUMBER

In Super Mystery Number, the player who is trying to guess the mystery number asks any question he or she wishes. Instead of using the card set with the questions, make a new set of ten cards with a number from 1 to 10 on each card. The other player writes a mystery number from 1 to 500 on a piece of paper. The player who is doing the guessing uses the numbered cards to keep track of the number of questions asked. The number of cards not used is the number of points earned. The first player to earn 25 points wins the game.

Division Scrabble

Play a game of Scrabble with division problems.

MATERIALS

masking tape
Scrabble game
marker
2 or more
players

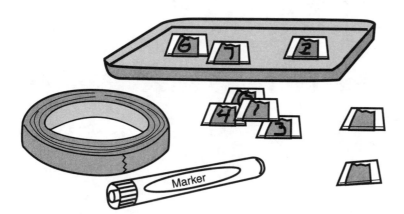

Game Preparation

1. Put a piece of masking tape over each of the tiles of a Scrabble game so that you can write over the ninety-eight letters and two blanks. Be sure to get permission from an adult before covering the tiles with masking tape.

2. On seventy of the tiles, write seven each of the numbers 0 to 9.

3. On fifteen of the remaining tiles, write a division sign. On the other fifteen tiles, write an equals sign.

Game Rules

1. Place all of the tiles facedown on the table and mix them up.

2. Each player takes nine tiles and places them on his or her rack.

3. Players take turns making division problems and placing them on the Scrabble board. Each digit, division sign, and equals sign is worth 1 point. For example, the problem $12 \div 2 = 6$ earns 6 points. The number 12 is worth 2 points since it has two digits.

4. Players replace the tiles they use by taking more tiles off the table.

5. The game continues until all the tiles are used. The player with the most points wins the game.

SUPER DIVISION SCRABBLE

Write both multiplication and division signs on the Scrabble tiles. Players earn points for both types of problems.

Divisor Here!

This noisy game for two or more players teaches you how to recognize the numbers divisible by a chosen number.

Game Rules

1. The players agree on a divisor. This chosen number can be any number from 2 to 9.

2. The players count in rounds from 1 to 100 or until someone makes a mistake. The first player says, "One," the second player says, "Two," the third player says, "Three," and so on.

3. Players shout, "Divisor!" whenever their number is divisible by the chosen number.

4. Players shout, "Here!" whenever their number contains the chosen number.

5. Players shout, "Divisor here!" whenever their number is divisible by and contains the chosen number.

6. If a player makes a mistake and shouts out a wrong number, that player earns a letter from the word *divisor*. A new number is chosen and a new round begins.

7. The first player to earn all of the letters in the word *divisor* loses the game.

Does it sound confusing? It is, but Divisor Here! is easy to learn and lots of fun! For example, this would be the correct sequence of answers if the chosen number were 5: 1, 2, 3, 4, divisor here, 6, 7, 8, 9, divisor, 11, 12, 13, 14, divisor here, 16, 17, 18, 19, divisor. . . . You get the idea. Since you don't need any equipment, you can play Divisor Here! in the car, on the playground, or anywhere.

BECOMING DAZZLING AT DIVISION

Now that you know the basic division facts, you are ready to learn more about division. The games and activities in this section will teach you how to solve long division problems, work with remainders, and estimate the answers to division problems. You'll learn how to do division problems in your head, and how to tell if a number is divisible by a given number just by looking at it. You'll also learn about fractions, prime numbers, and more. By the end of the chapter, you'll know so much about division that you'll dazzle your friends and teachers.

Flip-Flop

If you reverse the factors in a multiplication problem, you get the same product. For example, 5 × 3 = 15 and 3 × 5 = 15. What happens when you reverse the dividend and divisor of a division problem? Is 6 ÷ 2 the same as 2 ÷ 6? Here's how you can find out using pennies and paper.

MATERIALS

pencil
4 pieces
of paper
20 pennies

Procedure

1. Solve the problem 6 ÷ 2 using six pennies and a piece of paper. At the top of the paper, write "6 ÷ 2," then draw two circles on the paper as shown.

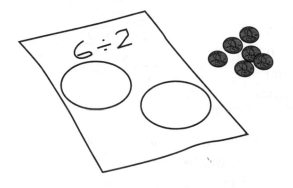

2. Divide the six pennies equally between the two circles. How many pennies are in each circle? Three, so 6 ÷ 2 = 3.

3. Now solve the problem 2 ÷ 6 using two pennies and another piece of paper. At the top of the paper, write "2 ÷ 6," then draw six circles on the paper as shown.

75

4. Divide the two pennies equally among the six circles. It's impossible! You only have two pennies, so you can't give each of the six circles one penny. The only way you could divide the two pennies into six equal groups would be to cut them up. Not likely! It should be obvious that 6 ÷ 2 is not the same problem as 2 ÷ 6.

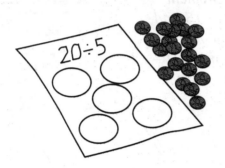

5. Is 20 ÷ 5 the same as 5 ÷ 20? Solve 20 ÷ 5 using twenty pennies and another piece of paper. At the top of the paper, write "20 ÷ 5," then draw five circles on the paper as shown.

6. Divide the 20 pennies equally among the five circles. How many pennies are there in each circle? Four, so 20 ÷ 5 = 4.

7. Now solve the problem 5 ÷ 20 using five pennies and the last piece of paper. On the top of the paper, write "5 ÷ 20," then draw twenty circles on the paper as shown.

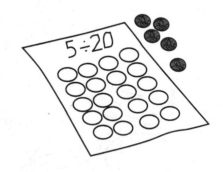

8. Divide the five pennies equally among the twenty circles. It's impossible! You only have five pennies, so you can't give each of the twenty circles one penny. The problem 20 ÷ 5 is not the same problem as 5 ÷ 20.

Division is not what's called "commutative." This means you can't reverse the dividend and divisor of a division problem and get the same quotient. So 12 ÷ 2 is not the same as 2 ÷ 12, and 15 ÷ 3 is not the same as 3 ÷ 15.

Multiplication is commutative, which means the order of the factors (the numbers you are multiplying) does not matter. The product (answer) will be the same. So $6 \times 4 = 24$ and $4 \times 6 = 24$.

You can even totally scramble a multiplication problem that has three or four factors and you'll get the same product. For example, $2 \times 3 \times 4 \times 5$ and $3 \times 5 \times 4 \times 2$ and $2 \times 4 \times 5 \times 3$ all have the same product. Multiply them and see!

There are exceptions to the "division is not commutative" rule. Can you think of a division problem where you can reverse the dividend and divisor and get the same quotient either way?

Whoops! Something's Left?

Every number can't divide evenly into every other number. What happens when you divide and you have something left?

MATERIALS

pencil
paper
25 jelly beans
or pennies

Procedure

1. What is 14 ÷ 4? Solve this problem using the repeated subtraction method.

    14 – 4 = 10

    10 – 4 = 6

    6 – 4 = 2

    2 – 4 = oops!

    You can't subtract 4 from 2. You can subtract 4 from 14 three times, but you have 2 left over. In a division problem, the number that is left over is called the "remainder." Fourteen divided by four equals three remainder two. You write this in mathematical language as 14 ÷ 4 = 3 R2. The R stands for remainder. Most division problems have remainders.

2. Another way to solve problems with remainders is to group objects such as jelly beans. What is 10 ÷ 3? At the top of a piece of paper, write "10 ÷ 3," then draw three circles on the paper as shown. Put a 1 in the first circle, a 2 in the second circle, and a 3 in the third circle. Under the three circles, draw a square and put an *R* in it.

3. Now take ten jelly beans and divide them equally among the three circles. You should be able to put three jelly beans in each circle with one jelly bean left. It's impossible to put the one remaining jelly bean in each of the three circles, so put it in the remainder box.

4. Now figure out your answer. How many jelly beans in each of the circles? Three. How many jelly beans in the remainder box? One. Ten divided by three equals three remainder one, or 10 ÷ 3 = 3 R1.

5. Use this same sheet with three circles and a remainder box to solve these problems:

What is 17 ÷ 3?

What is 22 ÷ 3?

What is 25 ÷ 3?

There is a third way to solve division problems with remainders if you know your multiples. A multiple is a number that can be divided by another number other than 1 with no remainder. Follow these simple steps.

- List the multiples of the divisor.
- Find the multiple that is closest to, but less than, the dividend.
- Divide the divisor into this multiple. This is the quotient.
- Find the difference between the dividend and the multiple. This is the remainder.

It sounds complicated, but it really isn't hard once you get the idea. For example, what is 7 ÷ 2?

- List the multiples of the divisor, which is 2: 2, 4, 6, 8, 10, 12, 14, 16, 18, 20, and so on. These numbers can be divided by 2 with no remainder.
- Find the closest multiple of 2 that is less than 7. Six is the closest multiple of 2 that is less than 7.
- Divide 2 into 6: the quotient is 3.
- Find the difference between 7 and 6. Seven minus six is one. The remainder is 1, so 7 ÷ 2 = 3 R1.

Use the multiples method to solve these problems with remainders.

1. What is 12 ÷ 5?

2. What is 28 ÷ 5?

3. What is 39 ÷ 5?

4. What is 46 ÷ 5?

Here's a clue. The multiples of 5 are 5, 10, 15, 20, 25, 30, 35, 40, 45, 50, and so on.

SUPER BRAIN Stretchers

See if you can solve these problems with remainders. Use any of the methods—repeated subtraction, grouping, or multiples.

1. What is $17 \div 2$?
2. What is $10 \div 3$?
3. What is $18 \div 4$?
4. What is $27 \div 5$?
5. What is $72 \div 10$?

Up and Down

*What happens when you divide a
number by several different numbers?*

MATERIALS

pencil
graph paper

Procedure

1. What happens when you divide the number
24 by 2, 3, 4, 6, 8, and 12? Is there a
pattern? Try it and see.

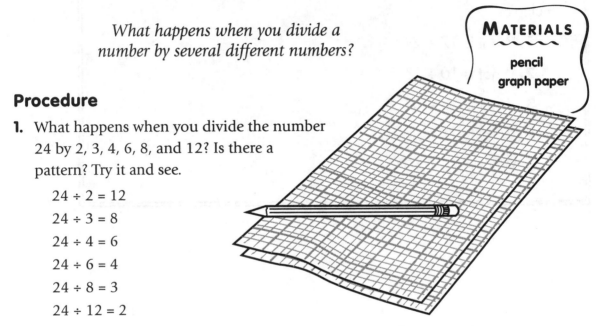

$24 \div 2 = 12$

$24 \div 3 = 8$

$24 \div 4 = 6$

$24 \div 6 = 4$

$24 \div 8 = 3$

$24 \div 12 = 2$

In all six problems, the dividend is the same: 24. In each consecutive
problem, the divisor increases, from 2 to 3 to 4 to 6 to 8 to 12. Notice
that as the divisor increases, the quotient decreases, from 12 to 8, 6, 4,
3, and 2.

2. Show these relationships on a piece of graph paper. Place a dot on the
intersection of each divisor and quotient. For example, for $24 \div 2 = 12$,
place the dot above the 2 on the horizontal (divisor) line and to the right
of the 12 on the vertical (quotient) line. Place a dot for the other divisors
and quotients in this way. Then connect all the dots with a line. This
graph shows what happens when the dividend stays the same and the
divisor increases.

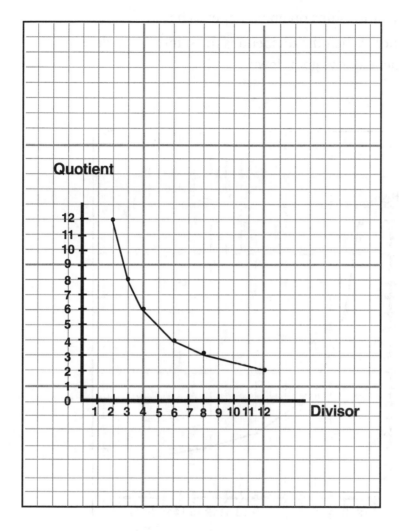

3. Does this happen every time you divide a number by several different numbers? Try it. Divide the number 36 by 2, 3, 4, 6, 9, 12, and 18.

$36 \div 2 = 18$

$36 \div 3 = 12$

$36 \div 4 = 9$

$36 \div 6 = 6$

$36 \div 9 = 4$

$36 \div 12 = 3$

$36 \div 18 = 2$

4. Now show these relationships on graph paper as before.

5. What did you notice? When the dividend is the same, as the divisor goes up, the quotient always goes down.

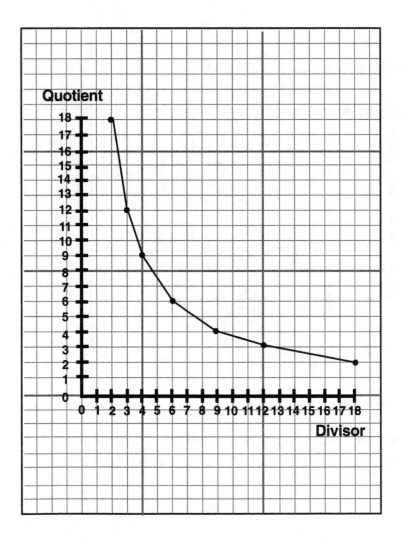

Look at these two division problems: $56 \div 4 = 4$ and $56 \div 8 = 7$. Both of these problems have the same dividend, 56. However, the second problem has a larger divisor, so it should have the smaller quotient. But 7 is larger than 4, so one of these problems is wrong. Check them: $56 \div 8 = 7$ is correct, but $56 \div 4 = 14$, not 4. It was easy to spot that one of these two problems was wrong, since the quotient did not go down as the divisor went up.

Look at these two problems: $100 \div 10 = 4$ and $100 \div 20 = 5$. Could both problems be correct? Why or why not?

What about these? Could both $120 \div 5 = 24$ and $120 \div 15 = 8$ be correct? Check them.

SUPER BRAIN Stretchers

1. What happens when you divide 10 by 10, 5, 2, and 1? As the divisor gets smaller, the quotient gets larger.
2. What do you think would happen if you divided 10 by ½? Since ½ is smaller than 1, the quotient would be even larger. So $10 \div 1 = 10$, and $10 \div ½ = 20$.

Solving Long Division Problems

How do you divide more complex problems, like 1,235 ÷ 5?

- You could count out 1,235 pennies, divide them into five equal groups, and count the number of pennies in each group.
- You could repeatedly subtract 5 from 1,235 until you get to 0 or a remainder, and then count the number of times you subtracted.
- You could make a long number line, draw arcs five numbers apart, and count the number of arcs.

But any of these methods would take a long time. It's much easier to use long division. Long division is easy. Just remember this simple rhyme:

Divide. Multiply. Subtract. Bring down.
It's so easy. Don't you frown.

A long division problem has four steps. You repeat these steps over and over until you get to 0 or a remainder.

1. *Divide* the divisor into the first one or two digits of the dividend.
2. *Multiply* the partial quotient by the divisor and place the product under the digits of the dividend that were divided.
3. *Subtract* the product from those digits of the dividend.
4. *Bring down* the next digit in the dividend. Repeat these four steps until the problem is solved.

This activity will walk you through solving a long division problem.

Procedure

MATERIALS

pencil
paper

1. Write the problem down in long division form:

$$\overset{\text{quotient}}{\text{divisor}\overline{)\text{dividend}}}.$$ Take the problem 1,235 ÷ 5.

This would be written in long division form as

$$5\overline{)1{,}235}.$$

2. First *divide* the divisor into the first one or two digits of the dividend. Can you divide 5 into 1? No; 1 is not divisible by 5, so divide 5 into 12. What is 12 ÷ 5? It's 2 with a remainder. Place the quotient 2 over the 2 in the dividend, in the quotient space. The 2 is called a "partial quotient" because you haven't solved the problem yet.

$$\overset{\displaystyle 2}{5\overline{)1{,}235}}$$

3. Now *multiply* the partial quotient 2 by the divisor 5: 2 × 5 = 10. Place the product 10 under the 12 in the dividend.

$$\begin{array}{r} 2 \\ 5\overline{)1{,}235} \\ \underline{10} \end{array}$$

4. Now *subtract* the product from the 12 in the dividend: 12 − 10 = 2. Place the 2 under the second digit of the 10.

$$\begin{array}{r} 2 \\ 5\overline{)1{,}235} \\ \underline{-10} \\ 2 \end{array}$$

5. Now *bring down* the next digit in the dividend, which is the 3. Place it beside the 2 you just wrote, to make a 23.

$$\begin{array}{r} 2 \\ 5\overline{)1,235} \\ -\underline{1\ 0} \\ 23 \end{array}$$

6. Now you are back to step 1 again, which is *divide.* Divide 5 into the 23: $23 \div 5 = 4$ with a remainder. So place the partial quotient 4 after the 2 in the quotient space.

$$\begin{array}{r} 24 \\ 5\overline{)1,235} \\ -\underline{1\ 0} \\ 23 \end{array}$$

7. Now *multiply* the partial quotient 4 by the divisor 5: $4 \times 5 = 20$. Place the product 20 under the 23.

$$\begin{array}{r} 24 \\ 5\overline{)1,235} \\ -\underline{1\ 0} \\ 23 \\ \underline{20} \end{array}$$

8. Now subtract 20 from 23: $23 - 20 = 3$. Place the 3 under the second digit of the 20.

$$\begin{array}{r} 24 \\ 5\overline{)1,235} \\ -\underline{1\ 0} \\ 23 \\ -\underline{20} \\ 3 \end{array}$$

9. Now *bring down* the last digit in the dividend, which is 5. Place it next to the 3 you just wrote, to make a 35.

$$\begin{array}{r} 24 \\ 5\overline{)1,235} \\ -\underline{1\ 0} \\ 23 \\ -\underline{20} \\ 35 \end{array}$$

10. Now you are back to *divide*. What is $35 \div 5$? It's 7. Place the partial quotient 7 after the 4 in the quotient space.

$$
\begin{array}{r}
247 \\
5\overline{)1{,}235} \\
-\underline{10} \\
23 \\
-\underline{20} \\
35
\end{array}
$$

11. Now *multiply* 7 by 5, which is 35. Place the product 35 under the 35.

$$
\begin{array}{r}
247 \\
5\overline{)1{,}235} \\
-\underline{10} \\
23 \\
-\underline{20} \\
35 \\
35
\end{array}
$$

12. Now *subtract* 35 from 35. The difference is 0.

$$
\begin{array}{r}
247 \\
5\overline{)1{,}235} \\
-\underline{10} \\
23 \\
-\underline{20} \\
35 \\
-\underline{35} \\
0
\end{array}
$$

13. There is nothing left to bring down, so the problem is solved. What's the answer? $1{,}235 \div 5 = 247$. You did it!

BRAIN Stretcher

Let's solve another long division problem: $2\overline{)607}$.

1. First *divide* the divisor into the first digit of the dividend. What is $6 \div 2$? It's 3. Place the partial quotient 3 over the 6, in the quotient space.

$$\begin{array}{r} 3 \\ 2\overline{)607} \end{array}$$

2. Now *multiply* the partial quotient 3 by the divisor 2. Place the product, which is 6, under the 6 in the dividend.

$$\begin{array}{r} 3 \\ 2\overline{)607} \\ \underline{6} \end{array}$$

3. Now *subtract* the product from the 6 in the dividend: $6 - 6 = 0$.

$$\begin{array}{r} 3 \\ 2\overline{)607} \\ \underline{-6} \\ 0 \end{array}$$

4. Now *bring down* the next digit in the dividend, which is 0. Place it beside the other 0.

$$\begin{array}{r} 3 \\ 2\overline{)607} \\ \underline{-6} \\ 00 \end{array}$$

5. Now you are back to step 1 again, which is *divide*. What is 00 ÷ 2? It's 0. So place a 0 in the quotient space.

```
      30
   2)607
    - 6
     00
```

6. Now *multiply* the partial quotient 0 by the divisor 2. The product is 0. Place the 0 under the second digit of 00.

```
      30
   2)607
    - 6
     00
      0
```

7. Now *subtract* 0 from 0. The difference is 0.

```
      30
   2)607
    - 6
     00
    - 0
      0
```

8. Now *bring down* the last digit in the dividend, which is 7. Place it next to the 0.

```
      30
   2)607
    - 6
     00
    - 0
     07
```

9. Now we are back to *divide*. What is 7 ÷ 2? It's 3 with a remainder. Place the 3 in the quotient space.

```
    303
  2)607
   -6
    00
   -0
    07
```

10. Now *multiply* the partial quotient 3 by the divisor 2. The product is 6. Place the 6 under the 7.

```
    303
  2)607
   -6
    00
   -0
    07
     6
```

11. Now *subtract* 6 from 7. The difference is 1.

```
    303
  2)607
   -6
    00
   -0
    07
   -6
    1
```

12. There is nothing left to bring down, so 1 becomes a remainder. The answer to the problem 607 ÷ 2 is 303 R1.

31

Three-Minute Long Division

Once you've mastered long division, here's a game you can play to show off your new skills. How many long division problems can you make up and solve in 3 minutes?

Game Rules

1. Player 1 rolls four dice of one color. The numbers rolled are used to make the dividend. The player may make more than one dividend by using any combination of two, three, or four of the numbers rolled. The digits may be placed in any order.

2. Player 1 rolls one die of a second color. The number rolled is the divisor. If a 1 is rolled, the player rolls again. The divisor must be a number between 2 and 6.

3. Using pencil and paper and the rolled numbers, player 1 makes up and solves as many division problems as possible within 3 minutes. Player 2 serves as timekeeper.

4. Player 1 earns 1 point for every problem solved correctly that has a remainder, and 2 points for every problem solved correctly that does not have a remainder. Use a calculator to check the arithmetic if necessary. For example, if player 1 first rolls two 2's, a 6, and a 1 to use in the dividends, then rolls a 2 to use as the divisor, these are some of the problems that could be made up and solved in 3 minutes:

$$12 \div 2 = 6$$
$$22 \div 2 = 11$$
$$16 \div 2 = 8$$
$$26 \div 2 = 13$$
$$21 \div 2 = 10 \text{ R1}$$
$$226 \div 2 = 113$$
$$262 \div 2 = 131$$
$$622 \div 2 = 311$$

With these problems player 1 would earn a total of 15 points, 2 points for each correctly answered problem with no remainder and 1 point for the one problem with a remainder.

5. Now player 2 takes a turn while player 1 serves as timekeeper.

6. The player who earns the most points in three rounds is the winner.

SUPER THREE-MINUTE LONG DIVISION

If you want to make the game harder, roll two dice to determine the divisor. The divisor is the sum of the two dice. Play Super Three-Minute Long Division the same as Three-Minute Long Division, except now the divisor is a number between 2 and 12 rather than 2 and 6.

32

Checking Division Problems

How do you know a division problem has been solved correctly? It's easy. You just need to know how to multiply.

MATERIALS

Procedure

1. To check a division problem, multiply the divisor by the quotient. The answer should be the same as the dividend. To check the problem $52 \div 4 = 13$, first remember the names of the three parts of the problem: 52 is the dividend, 4 is the divisor, and 13 is the quotient. Now multiply the divisor by the quotient: $4 \times 13 = 52$. So the division problem $52 \div 4 = 13$ is solved correctly.

2. Now check this problem to see if it is solved correctly: $144 \div 9 = 16$. Multiply the divisor by the quotient: $9 \times 16 = 144$. The problem is solved correctly, since 144 is the same as the dividend.

3. Now check this problem: $235 \div 5 = 54$. Multiply 5×54. The answer is 270. The problem is solved *incorrectly*, since 270 is *not* the dividend.

Try to solve the division problem correctly: $235 \div 5 = 47$. Now check your arithmetic. Multiply 5×47. The answer is 235, which is the same as the dividend. The problem is solved correctly.

4. How do you check a problem with a remainder? First multiply the quotient by the divisor, then add the remainder. Your answer should be the same as the dividend. Is $97 \div 3 = 32$ R1 solved correctly? Start by multiplying 3×32. The answer is 96. Now add the remainder: $96 + 1 = 97$. The answer is the same as the dividend, so the problem is solved correctly.

5. Now check the problem $618 \div 4 = 154$ R2. First multiply 4×154, which is 616. Now add the remainder: $616 + 2 = 618$. Since 618 is the same as the dividend, the problem is solved correctly.

33

Check It Out!

Now that you know how to check division problems, you can play this simple game of division chance.

MATERIALS

pencil
20 index cards
coin
several sheets
of paper
2 or
more players

Game Preparation

On each of the index cards, write one of these twenty division problems. Some are solved correctly and some are solved incorrectly.

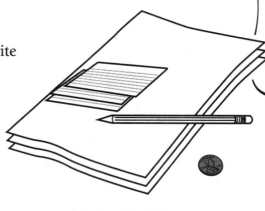

426 ÷ 9 = 44	1,134 ÷ 7 = 162
380 ÷ 4 = 95	2,472 ÷ 7 = 275
120 ÷ 3 = 40	966 ÷ 6 = 161
677 ÷ 9 = 115	566 ÷ 6 = 92
840 ÷ 2 = 420	770 ÷ 5 = 154
630 ÷ 5 = 126	648 ÷ 4 = 162
177 ÷ 6 = 28	728 ÷ 4 = 188
166 ÷ 7 = 28	927 ÷ 3 = 309
782 ÷ 4 = 190	150 ÷ 2 = 75
112 ÷ 8 = 14	680 ÷ 8 = 79

Game Rules

1. Shuffle the cards and spread them out facedown on the table.

2. Player 1 flips a coin. If the coin reads heads, he or she has to find a problem that is solved correctly. If the coin reads tails, he or she has to find a problem that is solved incorrectly.

3. Player 1 turns a card over and checks it, using pencil and paper to determine if it is solved correctly. If the problem is solved correctly and the player rolled heads, or if the problem is solved incorrectly and the player rolled tails, the player gets to keep the card. But if the problem is solved correctly and the player rolled tails, or if the problem is solved incorrectly and the player rolled heads, the card is turned over and placed facedown on the table.

4. Player 2 takes a turn. When there are no more cards on the table, the player with the most cards wins.

34

Ten-Second Guess Division

Guessing, or estimating, the answers to difficult division problems is good practice and makes a fun game.

MATERIALS

pencil
64 index cards
timer or clock with second hand
calculator
2 players

Game Preparation

Write one of the following problems on each of thirty-two index cards.

642 ÷ 2	118 ÷ 2	356 ÷ 2	894 ÷ 2
333 ÷ 3	894 ÷ 3	516 ÷ 3	114 ÷ 3
128 ÷ 4	724 ÷ 4	916 ÷ 4	424 ÷ 4
305 ÷ 5	620 ÷ 5	905 ÷ 5	105 ÷ 5
666 ÷ 6	234 ÷ 6	888 ÷ 6	954 ÷ 6
826 ÷ 7	119 ÷ 7	561 ÷ 7	348 ÷ 7
112 ÷ 8	344 ÷ 8	592 ÷ 8	776 ÷ 8
108 ÷ 9	414 ÷ 9	603 ÷ 9	819 ÷ 9

Game Rules

1. Shuffle the cards and place them facedown in the center of the table.

2. One player turns the top card over. The other player sets the timer for 10 seconds.

3. Both players try to guess the answer within 10 seconds. Players cannot use pencil and paper.

4. The correct answer is determined using a calculator. The player who comes closest to the correct answer without going over it wins the card.

5. When all the cards are gone, the player with the most cards wins the game.

6. Collect the cards, shuffle them, and play again. Make a new set of cards with problems that are a three-digit dividend divided by a one-digit divisor.

TWO-DIGIT GUESS DIVISION

Make a new set of thirty-two cards to play Ten-Second Guess Division. This time, make each of the problems a three-digit dividend divided by a two-digit divisor, like $222 \div 42$. Use the same rules to play.

THREE-DIGIT GUESS DIVISION

Make a new set of thirty-two cards with even more difficult problems. Each problem should be a four-digit dividend divided by a three-digit divisor, like $2,345 \div 321$. Use the same rules to play. The problems may seem hard at first, but with a little practice you'll get to be a pretty accurate guesser.

Daring Divisibility

How can you tell if a number is divisible by a given number?

Game Preparation

1. Remove all the face cards (kings, queens, jacks) and jokers from a deck of playing cards. You should now have forty cards.

2. Fold two pieces of paper into eight sections each. Cut the pieces of paper into sixteen small slips using the fold lines as a guide. On each of two slips of paper, write one of the numbers from 2 to 9, so that you have two slips with each number. Now fold the slips of paper so that you cannot see the numbers, and place them in a bowl.

3. At the top of another piece of paper, write "Daring Divisibility." Below that, write the names of the players. This is your score card.

Game Rules

1. Shuffle the playing cards and place them facedown in a stack in the center of the table.

2. Roll the die to see which player goes first. The player who rolls the highest number goes first.

3. Player 1 turns the top three cards over. The numbers on the cards will be used to make the dividend. (Aces count as 1's.)

4. Player 1 then draws a slip of paper from the bowl. The number on the paper is the divisor.

5. Player 2 is the timekeeper. Player 1 now has 1 minute to arrange the three cards so that the dividend is divisible by the divisor. (Remember, a number is "divisible" by another number if there is no remainder.) The player does not have to solve the problem; he or she only has to find a number that is divisible by the divisor.

6. Player 2 checks the divisibility of the dividend using a calculator. If the quotient does not include a decimal fraction, then the dividend is divisible by the divisor. The player earns 1 point.

7. Player 2 takes a turn while player 1 serves as timekeeper and checks the divisibility on a calculator.

8. When all the cards have been played, shuffle them again so that the game can continue. The game is over when the slips in the bowl are gone. The player with the most points wins.

There are shortcuts to determine divisibility.

1. Every number is divisible by **1**.

2. Every number that ends in a 0, 2, 4, 6, or 8 is divisible by **2**. In other words, every even number is divisible by 2.

3. If the sum of the digits of a number is divisible by 3, the number also is divisible by the **3**.

4. It the last two digits of a number are divisible by 4, the number also is divisible by **4**.

5. If a number ends in 0 or 5, it is divisible by **5**.

6. If a number is divisible by both 2 and 3, it is divisible by **6**.

7. There is no rule for determining divisibility by **7**.

8. If the last three digits of a number are divisible by 8, the number also is divisible by **8**.

9. If the sum of the digits of a number is divisible by 9, the number also is divisible by **9**.

10. If a number ends in 0, it is divisible by **10**.

SUPER BRAIN Stretchers

1. Use the shortcuts for determining divisibility to determine if 35,790 is divisible by 1, 2, 3, 4, 5, 6, 8, 9, or 10.
2. Use the shortcuts to determine if 9,360,351 is divisible by 2, 3, 5, 8, or 9.
3. What numbers is 605,248 divisible by?
4. What about 5,400?

36

Prime!

A prime number is a number that is not divisible by any number but itself and 1. Play this game to get to know some of the prime numbers.

Game Preparation

Write a number from 2 to 51 on each of fifty index cards.

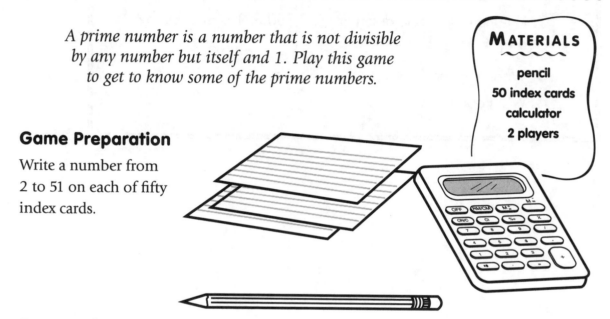

Game Rules

1. Shuffle the cards and deal each player half of the cards.

2. Players place their cards facedown on the table in front of them.

3. Player 1 turns his or her top card over and places it faceup in the center of the table. If the number on the card is a prime number, the first player to shout, "Prime!" wins the card. If the number is not prime and a player incorrectly shouts, "Prime!" the other player wins the card.

4. Use a calculator to check whether the number is prime. Try dividing the number by numbers other than itself and 1. If there is always a remainder, the number is prime.

5. Player 2 takes a turn with one of his or her cards. If the number on the card is prime, the first player to shout, "Prime!" wins the card and any cards under it. If a player incorrectly shouts, "Prime!" the other player wins the cards.

6. After all of the cards have been played, the player with the most cards wins the game.

BRAIN Stretcher

The prime numbers less than 51 are 2, 3, 5, 7, 11, 13, 17, 19, 23, 29, 31, 37, 41, 43, and 47. Try dividing these by other numbers (except themselves and 1), using a calculator, to see that this is true. Can you think of some prime numbers that are greater than 51?

37

Prime Mania

Learn division facts using prime numbers.

MATERIALS

pencil
8 index cards
2 players

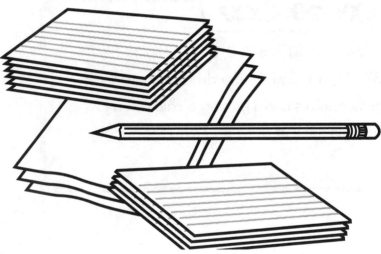

Game Preparation

Write a number from 2 to 9 on each of eight index cards. These numbers will be used as divisors.

Game Rules

1. Spread the eight divisor cards faceup on the table.

2. Player 1 thinks of a number from 1 to 100 and says it out loud.

3. If the number can be divided by the number on one of the cards, player 2 picks that card up, says the quotient of the division problem, and keeps the card. If the quotient is divisible by one of the remaining cards, player

2 picks that card up and states the quotient. If the quotient is a prime number, player 2 adds 7 to the quotient and states the sum. The sum is now the new quotient.

4. If the new quotient can be divided by the number on one of the divisor cards on the table, player 1 picks the divisor card up, states the quotient of that problem and keeps the card. If the quotient is prime, player 1 adds 7 to it to get a new quotient. If it is not prime, and it is not divisible by any number on the table, then the round is over.

5. The player holding the most cards when the round is over wins the round. The first player to win three rounds wins the game.

38

Back and Forth

What happens when the divisor is bigger than the dividend? What is 2 ÷ 4? Think of this problem as dividing two pieces of toast among four people. How do you do it?

MATERIALS

16 slices of toast
12 plates

Procedure

1. Set the table for four imaginary guests and bring out two slices of toast. If you try to give each guest one slice of toast, two guests will have none. When you divide, each guest has to receive an equal share. To give the four guests each an equal share, you will have to cut each of two slices of toast in half to get four pieces. Now give each guest half a slice of toast. So 2 ÷ 4 = ¹/₂.

2. What is 2 ÷ 8? Or how do you divide two slices of toast among eight guests? Set the table for eight. If you give each guest one slice of toast, six will have none. Cut each of two slices of toast in fourths to get eight pieces altogether. Now give each guest one-fourth a slice of toast. So 2 ÷ 8 = ¹/₄.

3. What is $4 \div 12$? Or how do you divide four slices of toast among twelve guests? Set the table for twelve. If you give each guest one slice of toast, eight guests will have none. Cut each of four slices of toast in thirds to get twelve pieces. Now give each guests one-third a slice of toast. So $4 \div 12 = \frac{1}{3}$.

4. Use the toast and plates to solve the following division problems:

- What is $3 \div 6$? How would you divide three slices of toast among six guests?

- What is $1 \div 4$? How would you divide one slice of toast among four guests?

- What is $1 \div 2$? How would you divide one slice of toast between two guests?

- What is $3 \div 4$? How would you divide three slices of toast among four guests?

5. What other problems could you make up using the toast and plates?

BRAIN Stretcher

Whenever the divisor is greater than the dividend, the quotient is always less than 1.

- The quotient of $2 \div 5$ is less than 1, since 5 is greater than 2.
- The quotient of $12 \div 20$ is less than 1, since 20 is greater than 12.
- The quotient of $16 \div 24$ is less than 1, since 24 is greater than 16.
- The quotient of $100 \div 1,000,000$ is less than 1, since 1,000,000 is greater than 100.

Fractions are really division problems!

- The fraction one-half can be written as $\frac{1}{2}$ and is another way of writing $1 \div 2$.
- The fraction three-eights can be written as $\frac{3}{8}$ and is another way of writing $3 \div 8$.
- The fraction seven-twelfths can be written as $\frac{7}{12}$ and is another way of writing $7 \div 12$.

Shout It Out!

*In this fun game, two or more players practice
dividing by the numbers from 1 to 6.
Speed as well as accuracy is important.*

Game Preparation

Write one of the following numbers
on each of twenty-seven cards:

2	14	32
3	16	34
4	18	36
5	20	38
6	22	40
8	24	42
9	26	44
10	28	45
12	30	50

Game Rules

1. Shuffle the cards and place them facedown in a stack in the center of the
   table.

2. Player 1 rolls the die. The number rolled is the divisor. The players will divide the number on each card played by this divisor. For example, if a 2 is rolled, the number on each card will be divided by 2.

3. Player 1 turns the top card over. All the players together divide the number on the card by the divisor. The first player to shout out the correct answer wins the card. If the number on the card is not divisible without a remainder, the players shout, "Remainder!"

4. If two or more players shout out the answer at the same time, the card is placed at the bottom of the pile.

5. If one player thinks another player shouted out an incorrect answer, the challenging player shouts, "Challenge!" and the answer is checked on a calculator. If the answer was incorrect, the challenging player wins the card. But if the answer was correct, the challenged player takes another card off the top of the stack and adds it to his or her winnings pile.

6. Player 2 turns the next card over and play continues as before. The players now divide the number on this card by the same divisor.

7. When all of the cards in the stack are gone, the round is over. The player with the most cards wins the round.

8. For each new round, shuffle all the cards again and place them in the center of the table. Let another player roll the die to get a new divisor. The first player to win three rounds wins the game.

Word Problems

Practice writing and solving word problems.

MATERIALS

pencil
9 index cards
lots of paper
large bowl
4 or
more players

Game Preparation

Write one of the following division problems on each of nine index cards:

24 ÷ 2	50 ÷ 5	48 ÷ 8
12 ÷ 3	84 ÷ 6	18 ÷ 9
100 ÷ 4	77 ÷ 7	60 ÷ 10

Game Rules

1. Shuffle the cards and place them facedown on the table.

2. Turn the top card over. Each player writes a word problem about the number problem on the card. A zany word problem for 12 ÷ 3 might be "Three friends shared a dozen chocolate doughnuts equally. How many chocolate doughnuts did each person eat?" The word problems are folded and placed in a bowl.

3. The problems are drawn from the bag and read to the group. Players vote on which word problem is the best. Players should base their votes on how interesting the word problems are and how appropriate they are to the number problem.

4. Each player earns 1 point for each vote in favor of his or her word problem.

5. The next card is turned over and players write new word problems. Play continues as before.

6. When all nine cards are gone, the player with the most points wins the game.

DIVISION MASTER CERTIFICATE

Now that you've mastered all of the division facts, problems, and games in this book, you are officially certified as a division master! Make a photocopy of this certificate, write your name on the copy, and hang it on the wall.

Division Master Certificate

Presented to

_____

for successfully mastering all of the division facts, problems, and games in *Dazzling Division* and achieving the honor of division master.

on _____ , 20 _____

Index

Index